SPELLING PRACTICE GRADE 4

THIS BOOK BELONGS TO

© Whiz Kid Books All rights reserved

Spelling Practice Grade 4 by Whiz Kid Books

Published by Alterra Business Consulting Ltd

Copyright © 2023 Whiz Kid Books

All rights reserved. No portion of this book may be reproduced in any form without permission from the publisher, except as permitted by U.S. copyright law.

Tips for Spelling Practice

Thank you for purchasing the Spelling Practice Grade 3 workbook.

There are 72 lessons with a total of 576 words. Each page contains 8 words for your child to learn. Some children will learn more quickly than others so it is important to work at the right pace for your child. Little and often is the best way to help them succeed.

Start by working together. Ask your child to:
- Read the word (help them if necessary)
- Learn the letters by repeating them out loud
- Copy the word, saying the letters out loud
- Remember the word, cover with a sheet of paper and write the word in the final column. See below.
- Check all the spellings and put a score in the box at the bottom of the page.

Lesson 1		
Read & Learn	Copy	Cover & Write
high	high	
every		
near		
west		

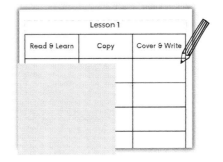

Lesson 1

Read & Learn	Copy	Cover & Write
rolled		
fingers		
except		
speed		
couldn't		
questions		
catch		
itself		
mark		
button		

SCORE

Lesson 2

Read & Learn	Copy	Cover & Write
bargain		
certain		
orphan		
fountain		
oxen		
latitude		
longitude		
compass		
absolute		
equator		

SCORE

Lesson 3

Read & Learn	Copy	Cover & Write
yourself		
maybe		
problem		
complete		
rather		
crowd		
since		
fresh		
piece		
cotton		

SCORE

Lesson 4

Read & Learn	Copy	Cover & Write
colon		
children		
heaven		
satin		
penguin		
commutative		
associative		
ecosystem		
community		
reproduce		

SCORE

Lesson 5

Read & Learn	Copy	Cover & Write
muffin		
pumpkin		
apron		
cannon		
poison		
landform		
prime		
composite		
wildfire		
tropical		

SCORE

Lesson 6

Read & Learn	Copy	Cover & Write
usually		
character		
friends		
whom		
heard		
order		
villain		
basin		
carton		
become		

SCORE

Lesson 7

Read & Learn	Copy	Cover & Write
twelve		
proverb		
across		
today		
during		
metaphor		
simile		
quiz		
however		
proposal		

SCORE

Lesson 8

Read & Learn	Copy	Cover & Write
rainforest		
bridal		
dental		
gerbil		
nasal		
postal		
hemisphere		
climate		
inverse		
population		

SCORE

Lesson 9

Read & Learn	Copy	Cover & Write
hours		
twenty		
products		
happened		
whine		
measure		
remember		
early		
utensil		
mortal		

SCORE

Lesson 10

Read & Learn	Copy	Cover & Write
vocal		
mental		
neutral		
anvil		
council		
abundant		
thrive		
canopy		
nutrients		
resist		

SCORE

Lesson 11

Read & Learn	Copy	Cover & Write
thirty		
synonym		
antonym		
usefulness		
covered		
anyone		
several		
juvenile		
reptile		
toward		

SCORE

Lesson 12

Read & Learn	Copy	Cover & Write
fragile		
hostile		
mobile		
tonsil		
evil		
terrarium		
depend		
destroyed		
resource		
factory		

SCORE

Lesson 13

Read & Learn	Copy	Cover & Write
byte		
extend		
keyboard		
monitor		
vowel		
portal		
tunnel		
against		
pastel		
numerical		

SCORE

Lesson 14

Read & Learn	Copy	Cover & Write
fatal		
oval		
towel		
chapel		
tinsel		
distributive		
compatible		
consumer		
producer		
pollinator		

SCORE

Lesson 15

Read & Learn	Copy	Cover & Write
vegetable		
tomatoes		
slowly		
potato		
carrot		
onion		
jungle		
crumble		
voice		
puzzle		

SCORE

Lesson 16

Read & Learn	Copy	Cover & Write
ankle		
freckle		
knuckle		
sprinkle		
dimple		
camouflage		
habitat		
hibernate		
mimicry		
predator		

SCORE

Lesson 17

Read & Learn	Copy	Cover & Write
thirteen		
appoint		
discuss		
demand		
request		
relief		
structure		
signature		
furniture		
departure		

SCORE

Lesson 18

Read & Learn	Copy	Cover & Write
culture		
creature		
fixture		
fracture		
species		
agriculture		
architecture		
view		
density		
capture		

SCORE

Lesson 19

Read & Learn	Copy	Cover & Write
fourteen		
plenty		
relax		
figure		
determine		
field		
travel		
sentence		
sketch		
rancher		

SCORE

Lesson 20

Read & Learn	Copy	Cover & Write
bleacher		
richer		
voucher		
pitcher		
catcher		
urban		
suburban		
rural		
estimation		
approximate		

SCORE

Lesson 21

Read & Learn	Copy	Cover & Write
forty		
English		
arithmetic		
half		
minus		
plus		
percent		
quarter		
finally		
zero		

SCORE

Lesson 22

Read & Learn	Copy	Cover & Write
fresher		
usher		
gusher		
crusher		
flasher		
balanced		
competition		
interdependence		
hypothesis		
endangered		

SCORE

Lesson 23

Read & Learn	Copy	Cover & Write
slide		
swings		
goal		
coach		
became		
shown		
minutes		
pasture		
adventure		
literature		

SCORE

Lesson 24

Read & Learn	Copy	Cover & Write
mixture		
moisture		
puncture		
sculpture		
carnivore		
herbivore		
omnivore		
photosynthesis		
echolocation		
lecture		

SCORE

Lesson 25

Read & Learn	Copy	Cover & Write
fifteen		
polite		
peanut		
soccer		
backpack		
decided		
contain		
course		
surface		
produce		

SCORE

Lesson 26

Read & Learn	Copy	Cover & Write
stretcher		
preacher		
pressure		
closure		
treasure		
pioneer		
immigrate		
migrate		
algebraic		
expression		

SCORE

Lesson 27

Read & Learn	Copy	Cover & Write
building		
spelling		
class		
fifty		
nothing		
revise		
carefully		
scientists		
inside		
wheels		

SCORE

Lesson 28

Read & Learn	Copy	Cover & Write
leisure		
seizure		
pleasure		
vulture		
rupture		
erratic		
moraine		
cirque		
monolith		
evaluate		

SCORE

Lesson 29

Read & Learn	Copy	Cover & Write
sixteen		
chicken		
elephant		
island		
gorilla		
dolphin		
machine		
ticket		
diet		
puppet		

SCORE

Lesson 30

Read & Learn	Copy	Cover & Write
banquet		
blanket		
gadget		
musket		
poet		
squatter		
strike		
exclusion		
watt		
fluorescent		

SCORE

Lesson 31

Read & Learn	Copy	Cover & Write
sixty		
system		
buffalo		
monkey		
alligator		
wolves		
kangaroo		
force		
brought		
understand		

SCORE

Lesson 32

Read & Learn	Copy	Cover & Write
audit		
credit		
hermit		
vomit		
habit		
bandit		
electrician		
mathematics		
mathematician		
renewable		

SCORE

Lesson 33

Read & Learn	Copy	Cover & Write
seventeen		
browser		
memory		
explain		
adage		
courage		
language		
luggage		
storage		
thousands		

SCORE

Lesson 34

Read & Learn	Copy	Cover & Write
bandage		
cabbage		
carriage		
damage		
garbage		
reservoir		
delta		
bay		
college		
university		

SCORE

Lesson 35

Read & Learn	Copy	Cover & Write
seventy		
rhombus		
equation		
average		
government		
filled		
pledge		
bridge		
ridge		
wedge		

SCORE

Lesson 36

Read & Learn	Copy	Cover & Write
ledge		
cartridge		
partridge		
porridge		
knowledge		
navigation		
circumnavigate		
globe		
public		
private		

SCORE

Lesson 37

Read & Learn	Copy	Cover & Write
object		
castle		
knight		
queen		
prince		
kingdom		
alone		
ghost		
robot		
program		

SCORE

Lesson 38

Read & Learn	Copy	Cover & Write
compose		
coastal		
soapy		
toaster		
owner		
entrepreneur		
boomtown		
compromise		
petition		
slavery		

SCORE

Lesson 39

Read & Learn	Copy	Cover & Write
solo		
duet		
material		
special		
heavy		
trio		
choir		
axe		
include		
homework		

SCORE

Lesson 40

Read & Learn	Copy	Cover & Write
lower		
bony		
stroller		
decode		
molten		
engineer		
technology		
electricity		
conductor		
insulator		

SCORE

Lesson 41

Read & Learn	Copy	Cover & Write
positive		
negative		
square		
syllables		
perhaps		
hammer		
nail		
suddenly		
chain		
wrench		

SCORE

Lesson 42

Read & Learn	Copy	Cover & Write
adopt		
bother		
congress		
comment		
monster		
parallel		
series		
charge		
export		
import		

SCORE

Lesson 43

Read & Learn	Copy	Cover & Write
hotel		
guest		
ready		
anything		
elevator		
generalize		
energy		
subject		
Europe		
umbrella		

SCORE

Lesson 44

Read & Learn	Copy	Cover & Write
bubble		
husband		
bucket		
publish		
snuggle		
inflation		
ration		
stock		
depression		
drought		

SCORE

Lesson 45

Read & Learn	Copy	Cover & Write
region		
return		
believe		
joined		
members		
contest		
reject		
cells		
universe		
computer		

SCORE

Lesson 46

Read & Learn	Copy	Cover & Write
abuse		
lukewarm		
salute		
rumor		
tutor		
actor		
magnetic		
poles		
permanent		
temporary		

SCORE

Lesson 47

Read & Learn	Copy	Cover & Write
eighty		
sherrif		
rodeo		
exercise		
wagon		
train		
railroad		
saddle		
calf		
developed		

SCORE

Lesson 48

Read & Learn	Copy	Cover & Write
alarm		
carbon		
charcoal		
marble		
scarlet		
aurora		
quadrant		
ordered		
coordinates		
grid		

SCORE

Lesson 49

Read & Learn	Copy	Cover & Write
window		
difference		
eighteen		
heart		
site		
burning		
corner		
harmfully		
curtain		
probably		

SCORE

Lesson 50

Read & Learn	Copy	Cover & Write
parsley		
tardy		
tariff		
prairie		
barrel		
ray		
dimension		
perpendicular		
intersecting		
quadrilateral		

SCORE

Lesson 51

Read & Learn	Copy	Cover & Write
ninety		
forward		
purple		
chord		
porch		
written		
purpose		
reason		
kept		
interest		

SCORE

Lesson 52

Read & Learn	Copy	Cover & Write
berry		
cherub		
merit		
perish		
mercy		
amendment		
principle		
citizenship		
convention		
responsibility		

SCORE

Lesson 53

Read & Learn	Copy	Cover & Write
nineteen		
score		
cousin		
present		
beautiful		
charm		
format		
portrait		
merge		
squirt		

SCORE

Lesson 54

Read & Learn	Copy	Cover & Write
sermon		
verdict		
bleary		
earthworm		
learning		
angle		
obtuse		
acute		
protractor		
vertex		

SCORE

Lesson 55

Read & Learn	Copy	Cover & Write
principal		
finished		
discovered		
amuse		
allowance		
beside		
concern		
thorn		
sword		
million		

SCORE

Lesson 56

Read & Learn	Copy	Cover & Write
clearing		
yearly		
career		
merely		
sincere		
translation		
rotation		
reflection		
tessellation		
symmetric		

SCORE

Lesson 57

Read & Learn	Copy	Cover & Write
kitchen		
dining		
pantry		
staircase		
instruments		
ornament		
shoreline		
storm		
afford		
raised		

SCORE

Lesson 58

Read & Learn	Copy	Cover & Write
burden		
purchase		
plural		
surgeon		
endure		
executive		
judicial		
legislative		
branch		
jurisdiction		

SCORE

Lesson 59

Read & Learn	Copy	Cover & Write
represent		
reply		
whether		
clothes		
flowers		
scan		
delete		
address		
describe		
stern		

SCORE

Lesson 60

Read & Learn	Copy	Cover & Write
mature		
obscure		
surely		
assure		
manure		
dirty		
curb		
radius		
diameter		
circumference		

SCORE

Lesson 61

Read & Learn	Copy	Cover & Write
actress		
theatre		
solve		
appear		
metal		
dramatic		
either		
neither		
goose		
village		

SCORE

Lesson 62

Read & Learn	Copy	Cover & Write
aloof		
moody		
raccoon		
askew		
jewel		
moose		
ounce		
professional		
millimeter		
centimeter		

SCORE

Lesson 63

Read & Learn	Copy	Cover & Write
factors		
result		
camera		
video		
image		
frame		
movies		
zoom		
cookies		
neighborhood		

SCORE

Lesson 64

Read & Learn	Copy	Cover & Write
flooding		
cookout		
footprint		
woodland		
mistook		
spooky		
perimeter		
irregular		
miniature		
artificial		

SCORE

Lesson 65

Read & Learn	Copy	Cover & Write
decade		
century		
outside		
everything		
release		
already		
instead		
phrase		
distraction		
completion		

SCORE

Lesson 66

Read & Learn	Copy	Cover & Write
affection		
collection		
construction		
fraction		
inspection		
inaccurate		
inefficient		
inoperative		
insecure		
illegal		

SCORE

Lesson 67

Read & Learn	Copy	Cover & Write
orange		
banana		
grapefruit		
pineapple		
strawberry		
laughed		
lemon		
quite		
type		
themselves		

SCORE

Lesson 68

Read & Learn	Copy	Cover & Write
protection		
reaction		
compassion		
adoption		
corruption		
illiterate		
illicit		
illogical		
illustrate		
immature		

SCORE

Lesson 69

Read & Learn	Copy	Cover & Write
temperature		
mirror		
breeze		
calm		
method		
section		
devotion		
infection		
within		
dictionary		

SCORE

Lesson 70

Read & Learn	Copy	Cover & Write
digestion		
disruption		
invention		
prevention		
suggestion		
immobile		
immoral		
immovable		
irritate		
irritation		

SCORE

Lesson 71

Read & Learn	Copy	Cover & Write
ribbon		
quantity		
amount		
scale		
remove		
although		
per		
broken		
moment		
invitation		

SCORE

Lesson 72

Read & Learn	Copy	Cover & Write
adaptation		
confrontation		
indentation		
plantation		
presentation		
irreconcilable		
irrelevant		
irreversible		
ecology		
astrology		

SCORE

Made in the USA
Middletown, DE
01 August 2025

11502757R00044